Grief

Grief

Recovering from the Pain of Loss

by

Granger E. Westberg

Marshall Pickering

To the memory of my sister Viola
who helped so many find hope
in the midst of grief

Marshall Morgan and Scott
Marshall Pickering
3 Beggarwood Lane, Basingstoke, Hants RG23 7LP,
UK

First published in the USA by Fortress Press
First published in the UK in 1988 by Marshall Morgan
and Scott Publications Ltd
Part of the Marshall Pickering Holdings Group
A subsidiary of the Zondervan Corporation

ISBN: 0 551 01623 X

Text Set in 12/14 Baskerville by Input Typesetting Ltd,
London, SW19
Printed in Great Britain by
Cox & Wyman Ltd, Reading, Berks

Contents

Introduction

We spend a good portion of our lives working diligently to acquire those things that make life rich and meaningful— friends, a wife or husband, children, a home, a job, material comforts, money (let's face it), and security. What happens to us when we lose any of these persons or things which are so important to us?

Quite naturally we grieve over the loss of anything important. Sometimes, if the loss is great, the very foundations of our life are shaken, and we are thrown into deep despair. Because we know so little about the nature of grief, we become panicky when it strikes us, and this serves to throw us deeper into despondency.

What ought we to know about the 'grief process,' so that we can better cope with it?

Does people's faith have anything to do with the way they grieve over whatever it is they lose? For instance, when we lose a job, or lose a loving friend, or fail in school, or are disliked by the people at the office because of our unpopular convictions, does our grief at these times have anything to do with our faith?

Faith plays a major role in grief of any kind. But not in the way some people think. They often seem to have the idea that a person with strong faith does not grieve and is above this sort of thing. Moreover, these people imply that religious faith advocates stoicism. They might even quote the two words from Scripture, 'Grieve not!' They forget to quote the rest of the phrase in which these two words are found: 'Grieve not as those who have no hope' (1 Thess. 4:13).

But religious faith—at least the Jewish-Christian faith—has never said that a truly religious person does not grieve. What it has said is that there are good ways and bad ways to grieve, and that what a person considers to be of most importance in life will definitely affect the way he or she grieves.

The theme of this booklet is really 'good, grief,' because we shall try to explore the good aspects of grief. We shall try to describe not only the pattern of grief, but also what we can learn from it. And since everyone in a lifetime must from time to time confront the loss of something or someone he or she loves, this booklet is for everyone.

If we include our 'little griefs' along with our 'large griefs,' we can say that grief is as natural to every person as breathing. It is inevitable! You cannot live without experiencing it in a thousand different ways. Such a seemingly inconsequential thing as your husband's phoning at the last minute, just before guests are arriving for dinner, to say that he has to work late throws you into a mild form of grief. Or perhaps the boss under whom you have worked happily for ten years is suddenly transferred, and the new one is pompous and overbearing. This is a form of grief. How you handle these 'little griefs' will in some measure tell you how you will probably handle the larger griefs when they come.

It is now possible to predict fairly well some of the things that will happen to all of us when some thing or some one very essential to our particular way of life is taken away. Before we describe the pattern which most of us follow, however, let us be sure we can picture grief in several more forms. We certainly mean to include grief related to death in this discussion; but we can observe the same grief process at work in many other kinds of losses as well.

For instance, one of the more common grief situations arises out of our mobile society where people move frequently because of change of employment or promotion. The uprooting of families has been going on long enough for us to be able to identify certain forms of emotional instability which result from it. The uprooted family is cut off from stabilizing relationships in the community which every child and adult needs so much. Every member of the family is adversely affected as they are rudely pulled away from people and things which have grown dear to them. There is every reason to raise the question whether corporations which transfer their key employees every two to five years are doing a wise thing, either for the family or ultimately for industry itself.

Let us look at a particular family that has been transferred three times in several years. They have lived in the present town for two years, and their children after some difficulty have finally found themselves in relation to their playmates and their school. The company now 'invites' the father to move for the fourth time. The mother in this family says that they have never before felt such a sense of belonging as they have in their present town. They had hoped they could stay there a long time. But her husband is on his way to being a general manager, and the company operates on the assumption that it is good for its executives to move frequently.

In the light of our new knowledge of psychosomatic medicine, we are not so sure it is a good idea. We who have spent years teaching in hospitals and medical centres see a great many sick or upset people who have come into the hospital in close relation to such an uprooting experience. I have seen children who are thrown into turmoil three months before the move and for three months or more after the move. Certainly such practices contribute to the instability of our society, and business institutions would do well to take a second look at the long-term results of such constant moving.

Or think of the problem of divorce. Certainly divorce is a situation which creates grief in the hearts of those who have now lost someone who once was dear to them. It is almost like a living death to see the one whom you continue to love turning his back on you, figuratively slapping you in the face.

Another form of grief may be retirement. Not all people look forward to arbitrary retirement at any age. They feel that they are good for at least another ten years. They hope their employers will make an exception in their case. But when that birthday comes, they too receive the summons. And many of these people leave their jobs with a heavy heart, having lost all reason for living.

We think of grief in relation to a man in his forties who is laid off indefinitely because of a business recession.

Then there is the person who has worked diligently to gain advancement, who has worked overtime and weekends to demonstrate ability to fill a particular position. After several years that job is finally open, and he is sure he will be chosen. But the boss remembers he has a nephew who needs a job, and the nephew takes over. Is this a cause for grief? Of course it is!

Another grief situation may centre around the children of a family. A child is lost not through death, but through marriage. He takes all his belongings from his room, and the house is lifeless. A house once filled with laughter and joy is now as quiet as a tomb. Or another child may turn against her mother and father and live her life in a manner completely contrary to their teachings. Or perhaps a student-age son or daughter who is deeply in love and making plans for marriage discovers his or her future partner has been untrue; and the wedding plans must be cancelled.

A list of losses would be inexhaustible. We can lose our health, our eyesight, our hearing. We can lose our home through fire or flooding or through financial ruin. In some families grief comes with the loss of a pet which has been a part of everything that has gone on in that household for ten years or more. Any of these things, and many more, sets in motion a cycle of grief.

Grief is a natural part of human experience. We face minor grief almost daily in some situation or another. To say a person is deeply religious and therefore does not have to face grief situations is ridiculous. Not only is it totally unrealistic, but it is also incompatible with the whole Christian message.

The one Bible verse every Sunday-school child knows by heart is the two-word verse 'Jesus wept.' These words describe a man who, when grief came, was able to weep, for He wanted and needed to express the feelings within Him.

But when we say, 'Grieve not,' then we imply we are to be Stoics like the Greeks of old. But we do not subscribe to the philosophy of the Stoics. Christians should

15

know the difference between Stoicism and Christianity. The Scriptures, both Old and New Testaments, see grief as normal and potentially creative. I suggest that in this eight-word piece of Scripture we put a comma after the first word so that it now reads, 'Grieve, not as those who have no hope,' and then I would add, 'but for goodness' sake, grieve when you have something worth grieving about!'

We ministers discovered some years ago that many of the people with whom we counselled were suffering from some form of sorrow they had not as yet been able to work through. As we began to try to understand the problems of our parishioners in distress, we sensed they were reacting to the loss of some precious relationship or possession in much the same way as people react to the loss of a love one through death.

We also began to sense that people in sorrow — from whatever cause — tend to follow a pattern which includes several stages. The idea of stages of grief was first suggested to us by Dr. Erich Lindemann, professor of psychiatry at Harvard University, who described the grief process in an article entitled 'Symptomatology and Management of Acute Grief,' years ago. In this remarkable study he demonstrated the difference between normal grief reactions and abnormal or morbid grief. He showed the importance of helping the grief-stricken person face up to the struggle of 'working through' grief. The person has to be helped to 'extricate himself from the bondage to the deceased and find new patterns of rewarding interaction.' He then described five things he saw in acute grief: (1) somantic distress, (2) preoccupation with the image of the deceased, (3) guilt, (4) hostile reactions, and (5) loss of patterns of conduct.

Dr. Lindemann's studies encouraged clergymen to deal more objectively with grief reactions in their parishioners. They soon found that parishioners who faced up to their loss by wrestling openly and honestly with the problem came through the grieving experience stronger, deeper, and better able to help other people with their grieving.

Of course, this wrestling with problems connected with loss also caused the parishioner to re-evaluate her own religious convictions. This meant that the parishioner began to question aspects of her faith and often went through periods of doubt in which she questioned the relevance of the Christian faith to personal problems. If, however, she was able to maintain some kind of relationship with God through regular worship and through fellowship with people of the congregation who really cared about her, then she looked upon the struggle as a growth experience which actually deepened her faith. Like Job of old, she was beset on all sides, but she refused to give up her basic faith. Through the centuries people who have been able to face grief in the knowledge that God still cares about them have said that grief can be counted among the great deepening experiences of life.

The ten stages of grief must be understood to be the *normal* process through which most people must go as they face up to their loss. In other words, we shall be talking about the road the majority of humans must travel in order to get back into the mainstream of life.

Now let us look at the ten stages of grief. Remember that every person does not necessarily go through all these stages, nor does a person necessarily go through them in this order. Moreover, it is impossible to differentiate clearly between each of these stages, for a person never moves neatly from one stage to the other.

STAGE ONE

We Are in a State of Shock

God has so made us that we can somehow bear pain and sorrow and even tragedy. However, when the sorrow is over-whelming, we are sometimes temporarily anaesthetized in response to a tragic experience. We are grateful for this temporary anaesthesia, for it keeps us from having to face grim reality all at once. This shock stage – or perhaps it should be called a counter shock – may last anywhere from a few minutes to a few hours to a few days. If it goes on for some weeks, it probably is unhealthy grief and professional help ought to be sought.

But do not be afraid of the shock that often comes in the early stages of grief.

Sometimes at the funeral home we see the sorrowing wife and find that she is almost radiant as she greets those who have come to offer their sympathy. People say, 'What serene faith she has!' We tend to equate faith with a social attitude, not with tears. Yet the truth of the matter may well be that this woman is experiencing a temporary anaesthesia which is helping her along until she is ready to move on to the next stage of grief.

The minister, upon seeing this woman in what at least appears to be shock, will arrange to visit her after the funeral, knowing that one day soon this strong exterior may break down and he will have to help her face her true self. In fact, in some cases he may even encourage her to break down and express openly the strong emotions she was not able to admit earlier.

A man who was unexpectedly fired from a job he had held for twenty years put it this way: 'I was so stunned by what they told me, I walked around as if I was in a trance. What they said just did not register. I heard the words but they had not "reached" me yet.' Shock is a temporary escape from reality. As long as it is temporary, it is good. But if a person should prefer to remain in this dream-world rather than face the reality of his loss, obviously it would be very unhealthy.

This is one of the reasons it is good for us to keep fairly busy and continue to carry on as much of our usual activities as possible during the period of crisis. It is certainly not good to have someone take over completely for us at such a time and make all our decisions for us at such a time and make all our decisions for us. Well-meaning relatives and friends might hinder the grief process by forcing us to sit inactively by. This would be much like the surgery patients in the past who were coddled and told not to do anything, not even turn over in bed for several days after surgery. All of this had the effect of prolonging the patient's recovery.

The same thing is true with grief. The

sooner the person has to deal with the immediate problems and make decisions again, the better. The personal tutor at a women's college at a particular university who has had much experience with girls at the time when they 'receive bad news from home,' says, 'I always make it a point to be right there near the girl the whole time she is making telephone calls and preparing to leave. But I always keep her as busy as I can, letting her do her own packing and making her own minute-to-minute decisions. The other girls in the house always want to wait on her hand and foot, but I've learned that this is the worst thing you can do for a person at such a time.'

To sum up: Be near the person and available to help, if everything breaks down, but normally do not take away from him the therapeutic value of doing everything he can for himself. This is what will help a person most to come out of his trance and 'get on with his grief work'.

Even though a person does come out of the initial shock, he will undoubtedly experience times in the succeeding days and months when the unreality of the loss comes over him again. Every now and then he will say, 'I just can't believe it has happened. Intellectually I know it did happen, but I guess I just have not really accepted it emotionally.' For all of us the biggest hurdle is 'accepting it emotionally.' We just do not *want* to believe it and so unconsciously we set as many barriers in the way as possible, making complete acceptance a very slow process.

STAGE TWO

We Express Emotion

Emotional release comes at about the time it begins to dawn upon us how dreadful this loss is. Sometimes without warning there wells up within us an uncontrollable urge to express our grief. And this is exactly what we ought to do: allow ourselves to express the emotions we actually feel. We have been given tear glands, and we are supposed to use them when we have good reason to use them.

In our society it is very difficult for men to cry, because they have been taught as little tots that boys do not cry. When a little boy falls and skins his knee and cries out in fright and pain, someone picks him up and says, 'Now, now, little man, don't cry!' And when he is eight years old and hurts himself, he does not dare to cry, nor at eighteen when something happens about which he ought to cry. At thirty-eight when some great loss is suffered, he *cannot* cry,

Many men think that crying is not only a sign of weakness, but that letting themselves go emotionally might lead to a 'nervous breakdown.' This has been disproven for years, yet men seem not to understand that it is the person who holds himself tense, who refuses to let go, who may be in for trouble. The Scriptures clearly show that when great calamities came to the hardy men of faith they wept bitterly; their 'tears were with them all the night long.'

When we speak about emotional release it reminds us of the whole subject of emotions and our faith. To some people it may sound strange in a day of scientific objectivity and coldness that we should encourage the expression of emotions. Are we saying that religion should advocate emotionalism? No, but neither are we in favour of an emotion*less* religion. Emotion is essential to a person and to try to repress it is to make one less than a person.

For us to imagine we can live fully and deeply without emotion is pretty ridicu- lous. We are not talking now about emotional*ism*. We are talking about the emotions which provide the motivation for everything we do. One of the great faults of intellectual Protestantism is that it has tended to stifle emotion. The Sunday services have more resembled a lecture series than a worship experience. We must not and we need not apologise for emotion in our religious experience; nor need we apologise for it in our grief. To bottle it up unnecessarily is to do ourselves harm. We ought to express the grief we feel. Some will be too embarrassed to grieve openly; but then they ought to go off by themselves and let their grief take its natural course in any of a variety of ways.

STAGE THREE

We Feel Depressed and Very Lonely

Eventually there comes a feeling of utter depression and isolation. It is as if God is no longer in His heaven, as if God does not care. It is during these days we are sure that no one else has ever grieved as we are grieving.

It is true, no one has ever grieved *exactly* as we are grieving, because no two people face even the same kind of loss in the same way. But the awful experience of being utterly depressed and isolated is a universal phenomenon. When we find ourselves in the depths of despair, as some readers may be even at this moment, we should remind ourselves that this is to be expected following any significant loss, and that such depression is normal and a part of good healthy grief.

One way to describe a depression is to say it is much like a very dark day when the clouds have so blacked out the sun that everyone says, 'The sun isn't shining today.' We know that the sun *is* shining; but it appears as if it is not. Perhaps you have had occasion to travel by plane on a day like that. Your plane climbs up and up through layers of heavy dark clouds and you cannot see a thing through the windows. It is as dark as night. Then suddenly your plane breaks through the highest bank of inky black clouds at twenty-eight thousand or perhaps thirty-eight thousand feet, and immediately the sun pours through the window. Everyone looks out upon the white billowy clouds still so black on the other side and some people exclaim, 'Isn't it beautiful!' Then someone says, 'Too bad the people on the ground can't see this.' But the people on the ground are saying, 'The sun isn't shining today.' The sun *is* shining, but something has come between the people and the sun. This is what a depression is like. Something seems to come between the person and God and between the person and his fellow men, so that he feels a tremendous loneliness, an awful sense of isolation. And he can't seem to break through it.

When we are depressed, we find ourselves thinking thoughts we never have otherwise. We say God does not care. We may even doubt that there is a God.

Depression is not something unique just to you or me; it is an experience that seems to come to all people when something they love and treasure dearly is taken away from them. In the Scriptures we hear strong men like David in the Psalms crying out in their isolation, 'Why are you cast down within me, . . . I say to God, my rock, why hast Thou forgotten me? . . . My adversaries taunt me, while they say continually, "Where is your God?" '

And deep inside it is as if we are saying

during the times when we are depressed, 'Where is *my* God?' Jesus himself faced this loneliness when on the cross He cried out, 'My God, my God, why hast thou forsaken me?'

What we must never forget about a depression experience is that one day it will pass. Dark days do not last forever. The clouds are always moving, though very slowly. The person in the midst of a depression is certain, of course, that the clouds are not moving. He is convinced that this is a state in which he will remain the rest of his life. Any attempt to try to convince him otherwise is useless. However, the experience of people through the centuries has been that the dark clouds of depression *are* moving; they *do* pass. One of the most helpful things we can do for a friend at such a time is to stand by that friend in quiet confidence, and assure him or her that this, too, shall pass. The friend will not believe us at first, and will tell us we do not know what we are talking about. We may even be asked

31

to leave. But the friend usually does not mean it. Once it is realised that our concern is genuine, then the quiet assertion of our own confidence in God's continuing care and concern will assist tremendously in the friend's recovery.

For some people the clouds roll away seemingly all at once. Something happens within them, or some important event triggers a movement toward the next stage of grief. For others it takes longer, stretching the weeks into months. Such people can be immeasurably helped by the constant, consistent concern of those who really care about them.

A congregation of religious people ought to live up to the well-known description of 'the community of the concerned.' If they are actually concerned about those who mourn, who feel lost from the world and from God, then they will earn the lasting gratitude of those who mourn.

STAGE FOUR

We May Experience Physical Symptoms of Distress

As a clergyman in a medical centre, where I have worked closely with doctors and their patients for many years, I have slowly become aware of the fact that many of the patients I see are ill because of some unresolved grief situation. Usually the patient first went to see the doctor with a physical complaint. In an increasing number of cases these people tell me about some great loss they have sustained during the past months or year or two. As we talk, it is clear they have not yet worked through some of the central problems related to that loss. I see this so often that

I cannot help drawing the conclusion that there is a stronger relationship than we have ever thought between illness and the way in which a person handles a great loss.

Some of these people who have physical symptoms of distress have stopped at one of the stages in the ten-stage grief process. Unless someone can help them to work through the emotional problems involved in the stage in which they seem to be fixed, they will remain ill. No amount of medicine will significantly change the situation.

Let me illustrate this psychosomatic problem by giving an example of the type of person I am talking about.

Here is a young couple in their early thirties, Mr. and Mrs. Brown, who live in a small town. They have a modest little home, and he works at a job he likes very much. His salary is small, but other things make up for it. He comes home for lunch every day, and his wife and he have time to potter in the garden together. Every day

at five he is home and they have all their
evenings together. Life is rich for them in
this community where both of them were
born and raised. They have their families
there. They happen not to have any children, but their nieces and nephews are in
and out of the house all the time, and so
they lack for nothing.

Then one day Mr. Brown is asked to
take his boss's place on a business trip to
a convention away from home. There he
meets a man who sees such potential in
Mr. Brown that he invites him to join his
firm, offering him a salary almost three
times what he is making at home. Mr.
Brown accepts the job, of course! Usually,
if you get an offer of more money, you take
it!

Everyone in their home town is proud
of the Browns because they have made
good. They are showered with parties and
gifts, as everyone wishes them well.

Mr. and Mrs. Brown move to a
beautiful house in their new town, and
everything is just as it is supposed to be

in the storybooks, except that Mr. Brown does not come home for lunch any more, and his wife misses him very much. Things go along quite well at first until they find that he frequently has to stay on in the evening to entertain customers at dinner. Mrs. Brown is not at all happy about this. But the real blow comes when they learn he is to be on the road two or three days a week. This means he does not see his wife from Tuesday until Friday.

What does this do to Mrs. Brown? It changes the whole pattern of her life. Days formerly filled with activity related to her husband, her parents and brothers and sisters and small-town events, are now filled with emptiness and boredom. All she has to do all day is face the four walls of this handsomely decorated house. By nature she is not an outgoing person, and she has never had to make her own friends, for they were already there. Her house takes on the appearance of a prison as far as she is concerned. She cannot help but resent her husband's new job, for it has taken him away from her. She even begins to resent her husband, for when he comes home at night all he talks about is business and how much money he is making.

Frankly, Mrs. Brown does not care a rap about the money or the success of his business. Secretly she wishes the business would fold up so they could go back to their old home. Of course, she does not dare say this. She has to put up a good front and pretend she is thrilled with her husband's success. Soon, however, this 'phoniness' begins to show up, and both of them sense that something dreadful is happening to them.

Mrs. Brown has suffered a great loss. She is a woman in grief. She does not confide in anyone, even by post, because it would sound so juvenile. After all, she is supposed to be thrilled by their new and better way of living. Yet she finds herself engulfed by loneliness, a sense of depression and isolation. Then she develops physical symptoms of distress:

headaches and backaches and all kinds of aches. Weeks go by, and she is miserable. Finally, she has to tell her husband about her physical symptoms, and he insists she see a doctor immediately. The doctor gives her some medication, and she feels better for a time. After a few weeks she has a recurrence of these same symptoms, and the doctor suggests she go into the hospital for a complete checkup.

In the hospital they find nothing physically wrong with Mrs. Brown. Still, she is sick, just as sick as a person with something like a broken leg or an ulcer. The doctor talks with a chaplain or a psychiatrist or social worker and asks him to look in on Mrs. Brown because he suspects this illness might be related to some family problems. At first Mrs. Brown talks to the chaplain only about pleasant matters. Finding him easy to talk to and not in any hurry, she then begins to say a little bit about how she misses her old home town. Gradually she breaks down and finally, with great emotion, tells the chaplain how she hates her husband's business, how she hates everything connected with this new move. Her hostility, her feelings of guilt, all these things are intertwined with her grief. This is essentially why she is ill.

In situations like this, where grief is so important a factor in the illness, we can see why doctors and ministers and others, such as social workers and nurses, must join forces so that more than just the physical symptoms can be treated. Mrs. Brown must now be helped to understand the cause of these symptoms. But more than that, she must be helped to work through her feelings of loss. The minister sees the 'working through process' as involving a re-examination of a person's faith, in this case, her way of looking at life. It is no small task, and it may take many months of discussion, self-examin-ation, study, and fellowship with the concerned community of believers.

In Mrs. Brown's case it might be that

her problem is related to the fact that she did not have the usual growing-up experiences which most people have at the age of eighteen or twenty. Her present difficult experience is a delayed reaction. Now at the age of thirty-two she has to face leaving home and family and losing her husband, all at once. The easiest solution would seem to be that he quit his job and then go back to their home town and live as they did before. But then Mrs. Brown's guilt would be compounded, for she would feel guilty of keeping her husband from a promising future. And now that he has had a taste of business success, we cannot imagine he would be happy in his former job. No, these people came to the crossroads and made a decision which forever changed their lives.

They cannot turn back and take up where they left off, because they are no longer the same two people they were before they moved on. They will never really be able to face the new kinds of problems which life presents until they have seriously thought through and reconstructed their basic philosophy of life.

Although Mr. and Mrs. Brown might never think of their problem as being at the core a philosophical and religious one, in essence that is what it is. Every man and every woman, in order to live a rich and meaningful life, must take a turn at being a philosopher, to search for meaning in living. This move with the new job has forced both Mr. and Mrs. Brown to rethink what they consider to be worth striving for. The Christian faith offers a stimulating context in which to do this rethinking. It is the desire of every good pastor to encourage people like Mr. and Mrs. Brown to discuss in depth such life-shaping beliefs, in order that their faith may develop a maturity commensurate with their chronological age.

STAGE FIVE

We May Become Panicky

We find ourselves becoming panicky because we can think of nothing but the loss. We try so hard to get our minds off the subject, and perhaps for a moment or two we can be distracted from our worries, but soon we are right back again where we started. Naturally, this hinders our effectiveness in anything we are trying to do. We find that our work shows we are not producing the work of which we are capable. We get to worrying about our mental health. When people ask us questions, we have to ask them to repeat so often that they wonder what is wrong with us. We simply cannot concentrate.

All sorts of unpleasant thoughts come

to us, as we recall people we have known who have had to go to mental hospitals after they have experienced some great loss. Inability to concentrate in time of grief is just as natural as it can be. It would be stranger still if we could easily put aside our grief for routine matters. When something has been terribly important to us for a long, long time and it is taken from us, we cannot be expected to do anything but be constantly drawn to the lost object and suffer daily as we struggle with the gradually dawning realisation that it is gone forever.

When a person begins worrying about losing his mind, he often panics. He becomes almost paralysed with fear. It is often fear of the unknown, or fear of something he does not understand, that throws him into this panic.

It is important that we understand something about the grief process in advance of the crisis, so that we may eliminate the panic that accompanies fear of

43

the unknown. When we have been briefed about some of the tricks which grief plays on our minds, then we are not overwhelmed by the disturbing thoughts that seek to take over. It is the panic of thinking we are going through something wholly abnormal that throws us deeper into despair. But it is not abnormal, it is normal! It is comforting to know that even panic is normal.

To help ourselves through such a period when we can think of nothing but our loss, we must be open to new and different human relationships. At a time like this all we want to do is run away from life. The last thing we care to do is to try anything new. We can think of a hundred different reasons why we prefer to stay home and be gloomy rather than go out and be forced to be nice to people and think new thoughts. Such an attitude is natural; it is to be expected. We must not, however, wallow in our gloom, for it will only prolong our grief work. And to work through grief is very hard work!

We Feel a Sense of Guilt About the Loss

At the very outset we should make the distinction between 'normal' guilt and neurotic guilt. Generally speaking, normal guilt is the guilt we feel when we have done something or neglected to do something for which we ought, by the standards of our society, to feel guilty. Neurotic guilt is feeling guilty all out of proportion to our own real involvement in this particular problem.

Let me illustrate real guilt or normal guilt. When we lose a loved one through death, it would be hard to conceive of any of us who had lived closely with the departed one who would not feel guilty about some of the things we did not do for this person when he or she was alive, or the things we did do that hurt this person when he or she was with us. We know we have sinned against this person by thought, word, and deed, and our religious training says we should face up to our sin, and we *ought* to feel guilty about it.

For the mature religious person guilt is not something new. In handling this sixth stage of grief such a person has some advantage over one who has never heard much about sin and grace. He or she has experienced the remarkable sense of release that comes when we admit guilt in the prayer of confession. Such persons know about the divine gift of forgiveness and acceptance, so they do not fear admission of guilt. They know that real guilt must never be glossed over, nor should it be repressed. They have learned to come to terms with it. And these terms include a sense of being alienated from God, genuine repentance, followed by honest confession. Contrite confession of real guilt is a part of every worship service. We all have need to say, 'Have mercy upon me, O God. Create in me a clean heart, O God, and renew a right spirit within me.'

There is also such a thing as neurotic guilt and it is often intertwined with real guilt. It is difficult ever to separate one from the other completely. *Every* person has some neurotic guilt feelings. It is a matter of degree. Everyone ought to be aware of these neurotic tendencies, and not be lulled into thinking that it is only the other person who uses such mental mechanisms to escape reality.

An illustration of neurotic guilt might be a daughter who has stayed by her aged mother's bedside in the hospital for days and days without sleep. The doctor now orders her to go home and get some sleep. This turns out to be the night that her mother dies, and she will never forgive herself for not being there when it happened. She broods endlessly about this and builds it up out of proportion to the real situation.

47

If only this daughter could talk over this whole problem with somebody who understands the deeper relations of which this guilt is but a symptom, she would begin to understand how to cope with her neurotic guilt and not have to be so unhappy. If she does not work through these problems at this time, they may hinder her full movement back into life again.

Unresolved guilt and misunderstood emotions of this type can make us miserable for years, or they might come out in a variety of physical symptoms of distress. It is important for us to face both our normal guilt and our neurotic guilt. We must not be afraid or embarrassed to talk about our feelings of guilt with those who have been trained to help us when the going gets rough.

We Are Filled with Anger and Resentment

Gradually we move up out of the depression, and in so doing we may be more able to express some of the strong feelings of anger and resentment of which we may not even have been aware.

When we say anger and resentment are a part of grief, we probably should qualify this to some extent. We do not wish to leave the impression that persons in grief ought to be encouraged to be angry or resentful. What we are saying is that these feelings are normal for every human, and that even the most devout persons can very well feel angry and resentful, even though we try very hard to sublimate these feelings. It would be most harmful to us if

49

we could not admit to ourselves, to God, and to our friends that we, being human, need to confess our anger and resentfulness and ask for strength to rise above it.

Another way to put it is to say that resentment is not a healty emotion and, if allowed to take over, it can be very, very harmful. Yet it is a normal part of the grief process. It is to be expected, it is to be wrestled with, and it can, by the grace of God, be overcome.

When we have something precious taken from us we inevitably go through a stage when we are very critical of everything and everyone who was related to the loss. We spare no one in our systematic scrutiny of the event, attempting to understand exactly why this thing happened, and who is to blame. The human is always looking for someone to blame. If we have lost someone through death, we express hostility toward anyone who cared for the patient. We are hostile to the doctor because he did not operate. No matter what he did, it as wrong. while we are in this mood, we look at everyone with a jaundiced eye. If we talk to the minister and are encouraged to admit what we really think, one day we may say, 'Why did God do this to me?' or 'How can He be a God of love if He treats people like this?' With Carlyle we cynically say, 'God sits in His heaven and does nothing.'

STAGE EIGHT

We Resist Returning

Although we may be quite well along in our grief work and really want to get back to our usual activities, something inside us resists returning. Our loss has been something special and we feel that other people just do not understand how great the loss was. They are off talking about other things and we are left alone with our sorrow. Everyone has forgotten our tragedy. Somebody has to keep the memory of it alive. We must not allow things to get back to normal again.

The pace of modern life may have something to do with this. The minute people finish one event they are off to another and another. And if they do not have enough happening in their lives, they live out other exciting events vicariously through television. Most people do not take time to help work through one another's losses. We seldom feel we have accomplished the work of grieving.

We also find, when we attempt to get back into life again, it is much too painful. We would rather grieve than fight the battle of coping with new situations. Grieving is painful, but not as painful as having to face entirely new decisions every hour. We are more comfortable in our grief than in the new unpredictable world. We want to stay with the familiar.

There are other related reasons for resisting the return. Our modern way of life makes it so difficult for us to grieve about any loss in the presence of other people. We are forced to carry all the grief within ourselves.

This is particularly true in the loss of a loved one through death. When many of us were children, people grieved more openly. The men wore black armbands and the women wore black veils for six months to a year while in mourning for a loved one, so that everyone was reminded daily of their loss. In some parts of Europe people continue to wear symbols of grieving. But we somehow have the impression that grief is out of place in our society. We conduct a quiet conspiracy of silence against it. We try never to talk about grief, and certainly never display it by any outward sign. We offer our sympathy to our grieving friends immediately after their loss has occurred, but from then on we say in effect, 'Now, let's get back to business as usual again.'

A typical illustration was the experience of a widow whose husband died a year or so ago who is with a group of friends who knew her husband. As they are talking together, one of them recalls a very humorous story about her husband. He is about to tell it, and then he thinks to himself, 'Oh no, I must not reopen the wound. I must be considerate of her.'

Consequently be carefully steers away from any conversation about her husband, as does everyone else. Actually, if he had told this story, she doubtless would have laughed heartily and been most pleased. He might have seen a tear or two in her eyes. If he had said, 'I'm sorry. I should not have told that story,' her response in all probability would have been, 'Don't say that! You are the first person in weeks who has even mentioned my husband. No one ever talks about him any more. It is a wonderful feeling to know that someone still remembers him.'

This is part of the task of friends – to help keep the memory of loved ones alive, to show concern for one another, and particularly when someone has suffered a great loss. Most people who are grieving are very considerate of others. They do not wish to force their troubles on other people. The quality of our personal interest in these people can demonstrate that we do want to share their burdens with them.

STAGE NINE

Gradually Hope Comes Through

Now and then we get a little glimpse of hope in one experience or another. This cloud which had been so dark begins to break up, and rays of light come through. We may be in deep grief anywhere from a few weeks to many months. We are never quite sure how long grief is going to last. We must remember that no two people are the same, nor are any two grief situations identical.

It would be wrong for us to leave the impression that we are less than human if we do not express our feelings overtly. Some people just do not express emotion and do not need to. Within themselves they probably struggle with many of these stages, but somehow temperamentally they are able to handle these problems very well by themselves. They do not need or want anyone 'meddling' in their lives by trying to help them through their grief. We soon learn, if we try to force ourselves upon someone like this, that it is better to let the person work out the problem for himself or herself and call on us if and when we are needed.

The great majority of us, however, need to express our emotions. We need the warm affection and encouragement of those about us. As we are the recipients of such affection, it makes it easier for us to sense that our present attitude of shutting out all new opportunities for meaningful living is unrealistic. We find that other experiences in life can be meaningful again.

The opposite of this is seen in the rich old widow who has acted strangely ever since her musician husband died twenty years ago. She has kept his music studio just as he left it when he died. She has locked the keyboard of his piano and has allowed no one ever to enter the room. Each day she stands for a long time in the doorway with her memroies. She has consistently refused to reenter life again. She is known by all as 'that eccentric old lady.'

Knowing what we do now about the grief process, it appears that at the time of her husband's death she was not helped to wrestle her way through to a new way of life. apparently, she had few or no friends who were willing to stay by her side during those difficult days, and as a result she had no one to encourage her to do her grieving in the normal way. She felt that her only friend was her deceased husband, and she had to remain loyal to him. That was why she locked the keyboard of the piano. She wanted no one else ever to play that piano again, lest she would be disloyal to the memory of the only person whose friendship she could trust.

In such circumstances one must seek out new friends who will help us to find the road to live again and who will walk that road with us.

STAGE TEN

We Struggle to Affirm Reality

We finally begin to affirm reality. Please note that we do not say that the final stage is, 'We become our old selves again.' When we go through any significant grief experience we come out of it as different people. Depending upon the way we respond to this event we are either stronger people than we were before or weaker – either healthier in spirit or sicker.

As I have watched hundreds of people go through earthshaking experiences of grief, I have seen that those whose religious faith is mature and healthy come through the experience in a way that makes them better able to help others who face similar tragedies. I have seen people develop a deeper faith in God as a result of their grief experiences.

Those who have an immature or childish faith tend to face the loss in a variety of *un*healthy ways. Some never really work through their grief, and months and even years later are still fighting battles within themselves. Persons who are spiritually more mature seem to be able to wrestle more effectively because they are aided by the conviction that God is with them. They do not feel that they have to face the present and the future alone.

I am convinced of the importance of keeping at the task of nurturing one's faith because I have seen how such people demonstrate greatness under trial. Conversely, I now have seen what happens to people who have not taken seriously the necessity of working at their faith when the going was good. These people seem unprepared to handle even the smaller losses which face all of us from time to time.

People of faith do not just suddenly get that way. Like the athlete who must stay in training, these people are always in training for whatever may come at any time. When loss comes they are ready for it. It is just one of many griefs they have learned to wrestle with creatively. They grieve deeply over their loss, to be sure, and they too go through the stages of grief we have described, but they eventually come to understand that *everything* has not been taken from them. They realise that life will never be the same again, but they begin to sense that there is much in life that can be affirmed. And to affirm something is to say that it is good.

At the time of great loss people who have a mature faith give evidence of an uncommon relationship with God. And they demonstrate an uncommon inner sense of strength and poise which grows out of their confidence that such a relationship with God can never be taken away from them. With such a basic philosophy they can face any earthly loss with the knowledge that they still have not lost everything. They still have God on whom to rely. I have come to see that this way of looking at life makes an amazing difference in the quality of the grief experience. It actually can become 'good' grief!

It is not right that people should try to carry on grief work alone. People through the centuries have found new and unexpected strength in the words, 'I am with you always.' So we say, 'Grieve – *not* as those who have no hope,' but please, when you have something worth grieving about, go ahead and grieve.

As we begin to struggle to affirm reality we find that we need not be afraid of the real world. We can live in it again. We can even love it again. For a time we thought there was nothing about life that we could affirm. Now the dark clouds are beginning to break up and occasionally for brief moments rays of the sun come through. And hope, based on faith in a

God whom our fathers have found to be dependable, once more becomes a part of our own outlook on life. Though we continue to struggle, we do affirm reality!